FOLLOW PRICE ACTION TRENDS

FOREX TRADING SYSTEM

By LAURENTIU DAMIR

TABLE OF CONTENTS

First of all, let me just clarify one thing. The "50 pips" you see in the title on the book is to be taken as an average. It does not suggest or guaranty that you will make 50 pips per day, every day. You will make roughly 50 pips per day, on average. Some days you will make nothing, some days you will make way more than just 50 pips.

On average, at the end of the month, you will find that you have come close to this goal, that the following material tries to accomplish.

Before you start to construct your trading system, you must first think about what is the trading style that suits you better.

Do you want to sit in front of the computer the whole day entering and closing trades on the 5 minute time frame or do you think that trading on a higher time frame will suit you better?

My advice to you is very simple and clear: always seek to trade on the higher time frames. It is easier to trade this way and it will make you much more money in the long term. If you are a beginner in trading, it is best for you not to day trade until you gain experience.

Trading on small time frames carries high risk due to short-term random moves that are almost impossible to predict. Not to mention that trading this way makes you vulnerable against economic news events that come out multiple times per day and usually have a big impact on the small timeframes.

Even after you get more experienced by trading successfully on the higher time frames and you think you are ready to day trade, my advice is to not trade on any interval smaller than the 30 minutes.

Moreover, if you do decide to day trade, consider it as a backup trading style, day trade only when there are no trade setups as per your system on the higher time frames. Always seek to trade on the higher time frame. Nevertheless, as I said before, if you are a beginner trader, and you probably are, I strongly recommend that you develop your trading system around a higher time frame like the 4 hours or the daily.

Forget about day trading for a while. Build your trading system and trade on the 4h/daily charts until you start to add to your account consistently.

COMPONENTS

With the above in mind, the next thing you should decide is what you will include in your trading system from the technical point of view to help you win as many trades as possible. Decide what will be the core technical parts of your trading system.

From my experience, I can tell you which are the tools that work best in forex trading, with a great rate of success. These are price trends, support and resistance levels, Fibonacci ratios, price patterns and bar patterns/candlestick patterns.

These are the things you should consider including in your system. They are the most popular things in the forex market thus, they have the highest rate of success.

PRICE TRENDS

You surely know what a trend is. You see them on your charts every day. The trend is a core principle of the forex market or any market for that matter and should always be considered when constructing your trading system. It is always easier to trade with the trend than against it.

A trend signifies that the majority of traders decided to push the price in one direction.

You must always know what that direction is and trade in line with it.

If you want to know everything there is to know about forex trends, how to spot them by reading the price action, how to recognize when the trend is changing without the help of any technical indicators, you can check out the book Follow Price Action Trends that explains this in great detail, with many chart illustrations, and puts it together into a complete forex price action trading system that can yield thousands of pips by trading these changes in trend.

SUPPORT AND RESISTANCE

Support and resistance levels are also a key component of the forex market; a large number of traders out there highlight them on their charts and base their trading decisions on them.

Therefore, it is advisable that when you decide to construct your trading system you take them into account.

FIBONACCI RETRACEMENTS

Fibonacci ratios are another forex tool that works extremely well in the forex market.

Just pull up any chart and draw your Fibonacci levels from the start to the end of any big move in one direction or another.

You will see how many times these levels act as strong support and resistance zones where price bounces back to resume the previous trend.

PATTERNS

Price patterns and candlestick patterns are also very popular with the vast majority of traders therefore, they too have a great rate of success.

Price patterns are used as signals that price is preparing for a move in a direction and candlestick patterns are used mainly as a confirmation when entering a trade. If you want to learn in great detail about all of these above powerful trading tools and master them, you can take a look at the Trade the Price Action book that explains them very well with many chart illustrations and puts them together in the form of an extremely powerful price action trading system. In conclusion, these are the things that you should include in your trading system because there are by far the most successful tools to trade the forex market. It is completely up to you to decide if you combine them all in your system or just use some of them.

There will be more about these powerful tools in a later section where you will learn how to avoid making trading mistakes when working with them.

NO TECHNICAL INDICATORS

Now that you have an idea of what would be best to include in your trading system you also must know what not to include in it.

Do not use any technical indicators in your trading because they are worthless, they will lose you money overall. You might win a trade today using them but you will surely lose all that money back and more by the end of the week. You should consider yourself very lucky if during one month you manage to break even by trading with indicators.

All indicators are based on past price action, the macd, rsi, or stochastic are not leading indicators. They are only leading you to losses. Being constructed of past price action they are all lagging. By design they follow the past price action, therefore, even if the signals they give would be accurate they are useless because they come too late for you to capitalize on them.

Always remember one thing: price leads the indicator, not the other way around. Do not be fooled when you do a back test on your charts and you see that using an indicator or a trading system with indicators would have made you thousands of pips.

That is just a trick. Real time trading has nothing to do with back testing. When you put that indicator to work in real time, you will soon see that you are wasting your time and money.

Always remember that price tells the indicator what to do not vice versa. The ultimate indicator is and always will be the price action itself. You should focus only on reading and interpreting the price action movements and not overcomplicate your trading system with useless indicators.

200 EMA

From my experience, this moving average is the only indicator that is worth incorporating in your trading system. It is the most important moving average of them all, all retail and professional traders keep an eye on it therefore price tends to bounce when it touches it.

However, it is best to use it in your trading system as

guidance, as a confirmation of what price action tells you and not as a tool to base trading decisions on.

For example, if your system is designed for the 4h chart, you will want to read the price action on that chart to know what the trend is. After you do that and see that the current trend is up or down, you can then look at the 200 EMA on the same chart to confirm and enforce your price action reading.

Let us say the price action trend on that chart is up. If that specific forex pair trades above the 200 EMA at that time on the same chart then you have a confirmation of your price action reading.

You can check out the Trade the Momentum book for a complete trading system that uses this moving average along with some other powerful concepts of trading to make 200 pips per week or more.

Let us see a chart with this moving average so you can

better understand how price reacts to it.

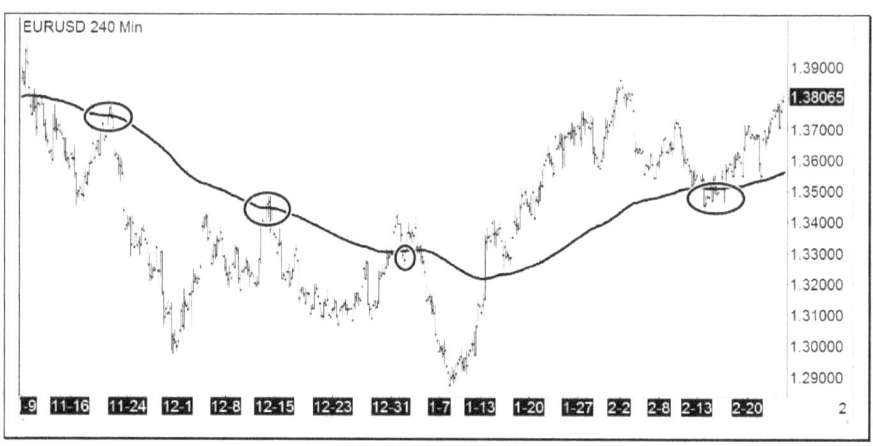

THE 4 HOURS AND DAILY TREND

A good trading system is the one that always refers to bigger picture. The bigger picture in forex is represented by the trends on the higher timeframes.

These trends control the price movement on the lower timeframes. If you design for yourself a system that trades on the 4h charts, you must always take into account the trend on the daily chart. If you trade on the 1h or 30minutes charts, you must always consider the trend on the 4h chart.

For the trend on the daily chart you can use the 200 EMA

discussed earlier. If the pair is trading above the 200EMA on the daily chart, it means that the trend is up on the daily chart. If the pair trades below the 200EMA on the daily chart, it means that the trend is down on the daily chart.

Therefore, any trades entered on the 4h chart according to your trading system should only be entered in line with the daily trend.

This is the way by which you can avoid severe losses and achieve long-term success. Let me show you a trade setup on the 4h chart generated by my Follow Price Action Trends trading system:

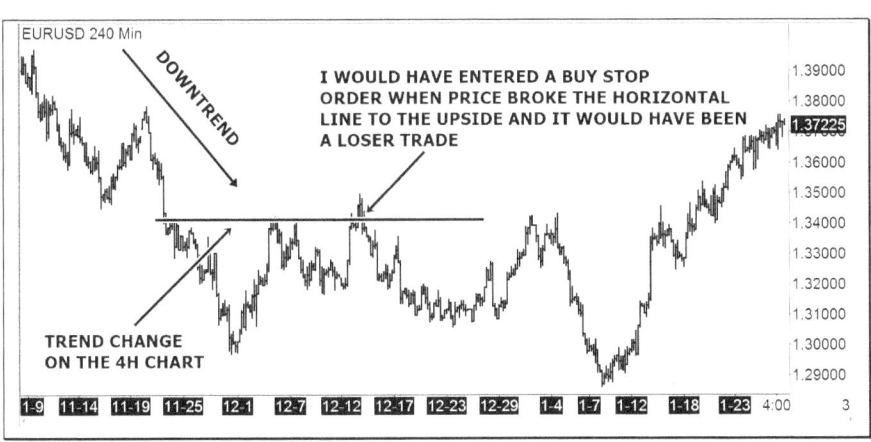

In the 4h chart above, a trade setup took place according to my trading system at that level where the trend changed from downtrend to uptrend on the 4h chart. I should have bought this pair at that circle in the chart.

Well, you can clearly see that price would have gone for a while in my favor only to retrace back down later eating all my gains and hitting my stop loss level. Is the trading system not good? The trading system is very good because it keeps me out of losing trades like this one. It always takes into account the daily trend. And the daily trend for that pair at that moment was:

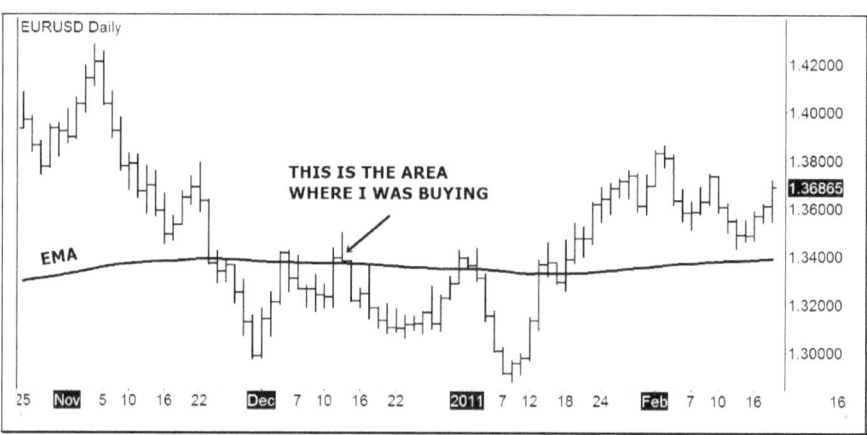

Well, the daily trend was clearly neutral at the moment when I was supposed to enter the buy order. The price action for that pair at that moment was below the 200EMA on the daily. You can see how price just touched the 200 EMA on the daily chart, creeped above it for a very short time period and bounced back down. As per my trading system, I would have taken this trade only if the pair had been trading above the 200EMA on the daily chart.

My trading system kept me out of this losing trade because it always looks at the bigger picture, yours should do the same. When you get more experienced and you want to start trading on a lower timeframe like the 1-hour or the 30 minutes the bigger picture in this case will always be the 4h trend. However, I do not recommend you to grasp the 4h timeframe trend just by looking at the 200 EMA.

The moving average works best to find the trend on the daily chart, for the trend on the 4h chart you will have to read the price action in order to get the best results possible out of your trading. You must determine the trend on the 4h chart by reading the price action, the moving average is not that correct on this timeframe and it can lead you to losses.

The smaller the timeframe, the less accurate the 200 EMA becomes.

The Follow Price Action Trends trading system teaches you with great detail how to spot price action trends on the 4h charts. In addition, the Day Trading Forex with Price Patterns trading system does a great job teaching how to correctly establish the price action trend on the 4h charts but with a different approach.

SOLID MONEY MANAGEMENT

The technical part of your system discussed earlier only solves half of the problem. The other half and equally important is represented by the money management component.

A very good money management technique gives you the opportunity to be extremely profitable with your system even if let us say, out of ten trades, five are losers.

Of course, if you build your system respecting all the rules above and the rules that will follow you won't be in this situation. If, for any reason you should find yourself in it, strict money management rules will make you profitable even in situations like this one.

POSITION SIZING

This is the first rule of money management.

For your system to be a good one, it must tell you how much money you are going to lose on a trade before you enter the trade in the market. To achieve this, you must first have a chat with yourself and think about what percentage of your equity you are willing to risk on a trade. My advice is do not risk more than 2-3% per trade.

Next, your trading system should give you the exact levels where you will enter the trade and where you will place the stop loss level before you enter the trade. Let us do the following exercise:

You have 1000$ in your trading account and you decided that you will only risk 2% of your money per one trade. This means that for the next trade you should risk losing only 20$.

Now, when a trade setup begins to take shape, you decide where you will enter the trade and where you will set the stop loss according to your trading system.

Let us say that you find out you will have a stop loss of 50 pips for this trade. This means that if the trade goes wrong and your stop loss is hit you should lose only 20$. You then divide 20$ / 50 pips to see the value in dollars for every pip that you lose. And that value is 0.4$.

This means that for every pip that goes against you towards your stop loss you should lose only 0.4$. Only after you have this value you determine your order size, which is a simple thing to do since now you know the pip value.

 This means you will have to trade with an order size of 0.04 lots (4000$). If you lose the trade: 50 pip stop loss multiplied by 0.4$ per pip equals 20$. You have to do this every time when preparing to enter a trade, always determine your order size this way, manage your risk, always put the bad scenario in front no matter how promising and rewarding the potential trade looks.

Don't you ever think about how much money you could win on that one trade. This will make you emotional, it will cloud your judgment, and you will be tempted to enter with a big order size to win more money out of the trade. Instead, always think of how much money you could lose and do the math explained earlier to determine the size of your order.

RISK-REWARD RATIO

Your system should spot trade setups where the reward is at least 2 times bigger than the risk for every trade.

This means that apart from the entry and stop loss levels, your trading system should tell you the take profit level also. You should know before entering the trade what is the risk and what is the reward.

If your system gives you trades where the reward is not 2 times greater than the risk or worse, the reward is smaller than the risk for every trade then it is not a good trading system.

You will lose your money in the long term. Whenever your system presents you a trade like this, do not take it, no matter how promising it looks. Let us do another exercise to see how easy it is to be profitable if you have a good system with solid money management rules: you have a system that gives you trades with 1:3 risk-reward ratio or more. This means that for every pip you risk losing, the reward is 3 times greater. If you enter a trade with 50 pips stop loss this means that your profit target is 150 pips.

Let us say that on a given month you made 15 trades according to your system, each of them with a 50 pips stop loss and 150 pips profit target. But, the market went crazy that month and out of those 15 trades only 5 of them were winners. 10 were losers.

Therefore, you have only managed a 33% success rates with your trading system, which is very low. Here is where money management shows its value.

Let us do the math. You lost 10 trades with 50 pips stop loss on each of them. This means you lost a total of 500 pips that month. You only won five trades.

With the profit target being 3 times greater than the risk, that is 150 pips won per every trade, this means you have won a total of 750 pips on that month. Therefore, you have lost 10 trades out of 15 which is dreadful but you've still made a profit of 250 pips on that month thanks to money management rules.

STOP LOSS PLACEMENT

Your stop loss should exist for every trade, but the stop loss must always be set at logical places in the market, not randomly. My advice to you is to always put your stop loss at the level where the price has very little chance to reach given the conditions of the market at that moment.

Let us see an example:

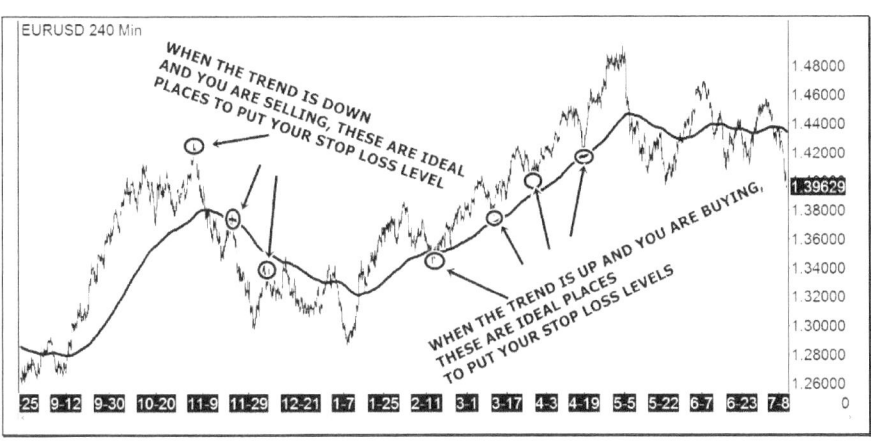

As you can see, when you sell, you put your stop loss just

above the swing highs that price makes. When you buy, you put your stop loss just below the swing lows that price makes on its way up.

If at the time your trading system gives you a potential trade you do not see a logical point in the market like these in the chart above, you do not enter the trade no matter how lucrative it might appear.

PATIENCE, NO EMOTIONS, NO OUTSIDE INFLUENCE

This does not have much to do with money management but it is very important and it has to be outlined. Without patience when trading in the forex market, you have only small chances of success.

If you construct yourself a trading system and 2 or 3 days go by without a trade setup you have to be patient, the setup will come, don't start to bend the rules and chase trades, there is no rule that says you have to trade every single day in order to make money.

Forex is about patiently waiting for the market to present

to you the perfect conditions for a winner trade.

Respect your trading system and trade only by its rules, the trades will come.

Do not be emotional when trading, leave your emotions at the door, and do exactly as the system tells you to do. If your system tells you that you have to trail manually the stop loss above every swing high but the trade has already gone 100 pips in your favor and did not make any swing high yet, wait.

Leave your stop loss at its original place; do not think emotionally, that you have to secure those 100 pips so you do not lose them. This makes you lose money. Completely disregard any comments from individuals on forex forums that tell you to buy or sell because they have the holy grail and they know better than you what is about to happen.

Only trade what your system tells you to trade, do not let yourself be influenced by anyone, no matter how convincing they sound. If you pay attention to some fellow that tells you to buy a specific pair, you will lose your clear and unbiased judgment and without even knowing, you will start to browse through the charts looking for trade setups that sustain that guy's theory and that have nothing to do with your trading system. It is your money; wouldn't you feel stupid if you would lose them by trading based on someone else's suggestions?

DON'T DO THIS

Now, after you finally construct your trading system according to all the rules above you must learn how to avoid making mistakes when putting your system to work.

PRICE PATTERN BREAKS

If your system includes trading price patterns, you must know that for a pattern to be considered broken price must close outside of it. If you have a trading system using price pattern breaks to signal your entry, then you must wait for a candle or bar to close outside the pattern on the same timeframe where you spotted the pattern.

Do not make the mistake to spot a pattern on the 4h chart

and then go the 15 minutes chart and wait for a 15 minutes candle to close outside and call this a break of the pattern. If the pattern resides on the 4h chart, you must always wait for a 4h candle to close outside with momentum, meaning that the candle should have at least half of its body outside the pattern to consider it a break. Let us see an example:

In the chart above, you have a descending triangle pattern. You can see that there is a candle that goes below the pattern but does not manage to close below the triangle at that first arrow there.

On the next candle, price quickly retraces back into the pattern. This is not a pattern break. On the second arrow there is indeed a candle closes strongly outside the pattern, with momentum; 3 quarters of its length are outside the pattern. This is a price pattern break. Even if the first candle that went outside the pattern would have closed at its low, that still would not have counted as a break because of the fact that it only went outside with less than half of its overall length.

If you are looking for a powerful trading system with price patterns and price action trends that can deliver more than 1000 pips per month you can check out my book Day Trading Forex with Price Patterns

CANDLESTICK CONFIRMATION

If your newly developed system uses candlestick patterns to confirm the trade entry you must always wait for that candlestick pattern to complete.

Wait for the last candle of the pattern to close before you enter the trade. If right at the close of the pattern there is some important economic news coming out they could invalidate your pattern and with it your entry signal. Remember that candlestick patterns work well because a lot of traders watch them and act on them. If you enter before the pattern completes and when the last candle finally closes you see that the pattern is not valid anymore then a lot of traders will not trade at that level because there is no valid pattern so you will be in the minority.

The minority always loses in forex. In addition, you have to know that candlestick patterns have their greatest success rate when found at price extremes. Let me show you what I mean:

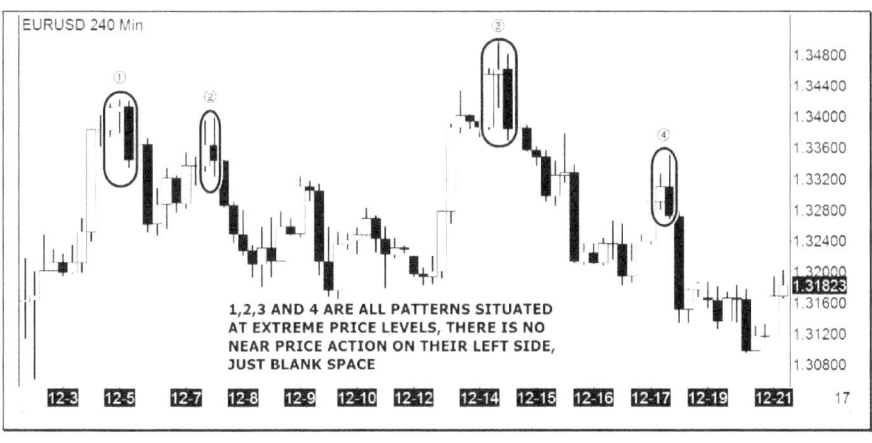

All the patterns in the chart above are situated at extremes of price. There is no recent price action at that level preceding them. These kinds of candlestick patterns have a very high rate of success. If your confirmation pattern takes place at a level where price action is trading sideways it might not be a very good confirmation signal.

FIBONACCI RETRACEMENT LEVELS

If you use Fibonacci levels in your trading system, then always wait for the price to touch the level you are watching before you consider entering a trade. Do not trade if the price comes close to your Fibonacci retracement level but does not touch it.

Let me show you what I mean:

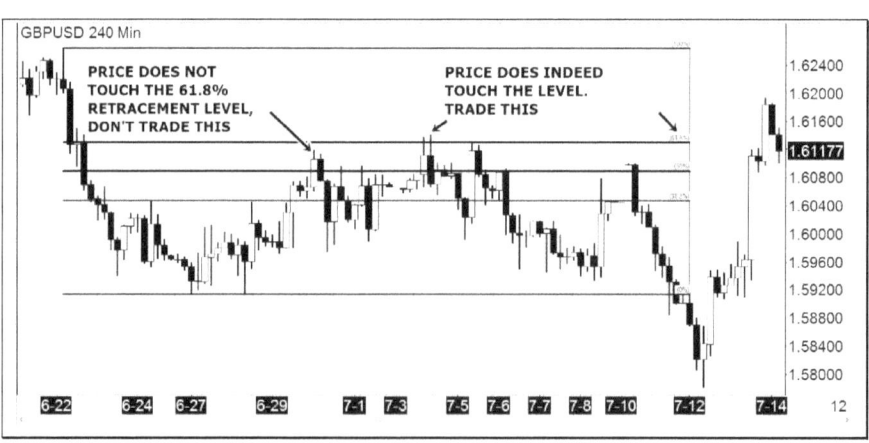

In the first attempt price comes close to the Fibonacci level but does not touch it.

It even makes a reversal candlestick pattern there suggesting that price will resume the trend down but soon after, price climbs back to the level this time touching and piercing it. This is the time to trade. If you had sold on the first attempt, you would have had your stop loss hit.

SUPPORT AND RESISTANCE

When trading with support and resistance levels make sure that you draw the most important ones, the pivotal ones where price bounces of them from either side.

These pivotal support and resistance zones are by far the most important ones they attract the most attention from the traders out there.

Do not beat yourself up with small, meaningless support and resistance zones. They are all over the place and they will clutter your charts for nothing.

Let me show you what a pivotal support or resistance zone

looks like:

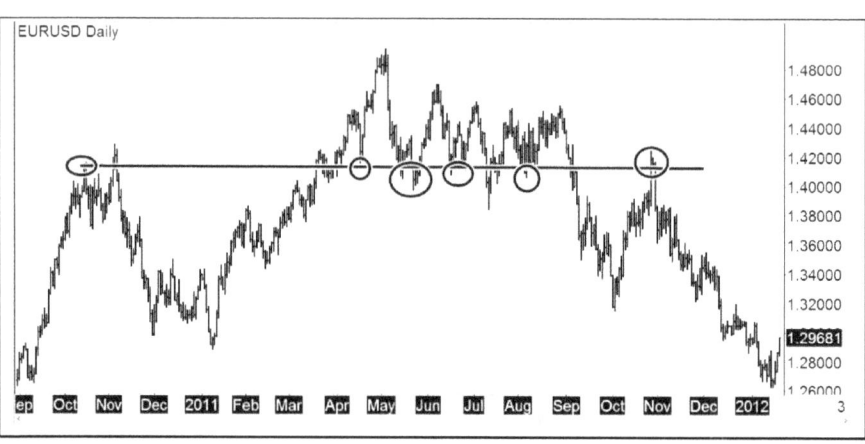

You can see here that price coming from the upside bounces 4 times off of the support shown by the horizontal line in the middle of the chart there, finally goes below it, and then starts to bounce off of it coming from below on that last circle on the right.

The horizontal line is now acting as resistance after providing support for a long period of time, on multiple occasions.

These are very strong support and resistance zones that you always have to keep an eye on. They hold the test of time, when price comes towards them, either from above or below, it will react to it.

CUTTING PROFITS SHORT

This is a very common mistake made by novice traders. When a trade goes in your way for 100 pips do not close it in fear that price will come back to the entry level and eat all your profits.

Respect the trading system's rules and let the trade run until it hits your profit target or until it hits you stop loss level that you manually trailed above or below swings in the market.

You will never make money if you keep cutting your profits short because you fear of losing them. How would you feel if after you close the trade with 100 pips in profit, price goes on further and hits your target level at 200 pips in profit?

LETTING LOSSES RUN

This is also a very common mistake made by novice traders.

When you see that price is going towards your stop loss, don't ever move it further away thinking that it is just a spike in price and the trade will go your way eventually.

The second you remove that stop loss from its initial place decided by the system you constructed you put yourself under great risk.

Accept the small loss and wait patiently for the next trade setup. There will be some occasional loses; no system is perfect, just because you had a loss does not mean that you have to change the system because there is something wrong with it.

Accept the small drawdown and leave the stop loss level in its place otherwise, instead of a 20 pips loss, you will quickly find yourself in a position where you have no choice but to accept a much bigger loss.

It does not matter if you lose one trade, as you have seen earlier, you can be profitable even if you only win 33% of your trades with solid management rules.

REVENGE TRADING

If you lose one trade, keep calm, do not think to yourself that you have to recuperate the loss right away.

This is the worst thing you could do, to enter the market randomly and with a bigger order size, not obeying your trading system, thinking that you must get back the money you lost otherwise you won't sleep well through the night.

This is called revenge trading, and it clouds your judgment so hard that you could lose all your hard-earned money in a single day.

Close the computer and go about your business. Tomorrow is another day and you will get the money back surely if you trade according to your trading system.

50 PIPS A DAY FOREX STRATEGY
COMPONENTS

200 periods Exponential Moving Average

Support and Resistance levels

Candlesticks

This is a clean, easy to follow, and extremely profitable trading strategy to get you started in trading and to put you on the path of consistent profitability. It is better to trade with this strategy on the 4h chart but you can trade it on the daily as well.

 The bigger the time frame the more important it is for the overall market movements, therefore, the more profitable your trading will be. It is very easy to understand and to put in practice immediately, anyone can do it if they know the basics of how the forex market works, what a forex pair is, and how to open and close an order.

 I will now try to explain how each of the three components helps us to win trades with this strategy.

The moving average tells us what the main trend is on the 4h chart. This is very simple to do, just plot the 200 EMA on your 4h chart and observe where the current price is situated in respect to the moving average. If the pair at the current time trades above the moving average then the overall trend is up, if it trades below the moving average then the trend is down.

The moving average itself must have a clear slope in one direction. This means that for you to consider that the trend on the 4h chart is up the moving average must be sloping upwards and the pair has to be trading above it at that time. For a downtrend, the moving average must have a clear slope down and the pair has to trade below it.

This diagram shows exactly how to spot an uptrend.

After we establish that there is a clear trend we then move on to the next level and we will try to find a support or resistance level.

I have told you that the moving average helps us to gauge the trend on a pair. If we find a trend, we go on further analyzing that pair to find a support or a resistance level, where it is most likely that whoever is in charge of that pair (the buyers or the sellers), will pick up the pace, and resume the trend.

The support/resistance level has to be a diagonal one and the trend line drawn on the chart to construct it has to be sloping against the trend.

You draw this trend line on your chart by connecting at least two distinct points in the market although three points will be better. Here is what I mean:

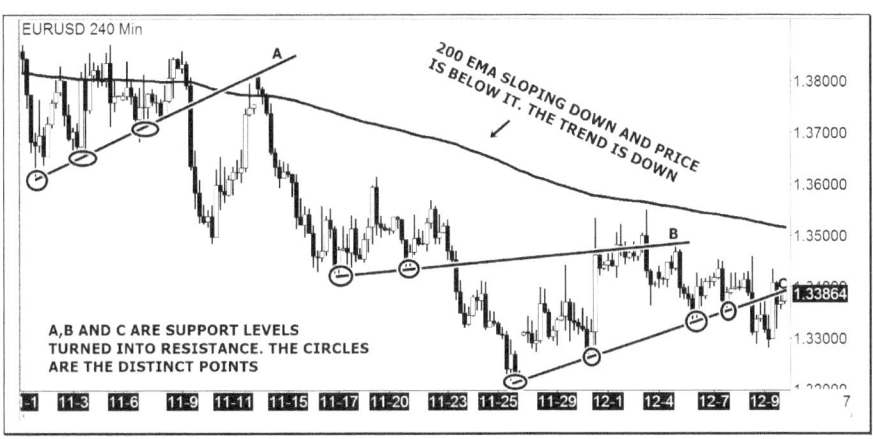

In this diagram, you can see that after recognizing a clear downtrend we move forward to discover three resistance levels one after another.

On the first one (A) we draw a trend line to connect the three distinct swing lows found there, on the second one we have only two distinct points, and on the third one, we have four points to connect with a trend line.

The more points there are to connect the better, the more important the support/resistance is. You can also see that all these three levels are pointing up against the main trend, which is a requirement for this trading strategy.

These three levels at first served as support for price action but once they were broken to the downside, they turned into resistance levels.

Now, about the third component of this strategy.

This strategy uses candlesticks to enter trades. After finding a clear trend and a support or resistance zone, you have to wait for price to go back to that support/resistance level and retest it.

This is where the candlesticks come into play. Before you enter a trade in the direction of the main trend, there has to be a candlestick confirmation that the trend is indeed resuming.

You will be looking for big body candlesticks that close at or near the high or low, which shows that there is momentum in the market and the dominant side (buyers or sellers) have decided to step in and continue the trend.

Let me show you the same chart above again to see what I mean by retest of the resistance level:

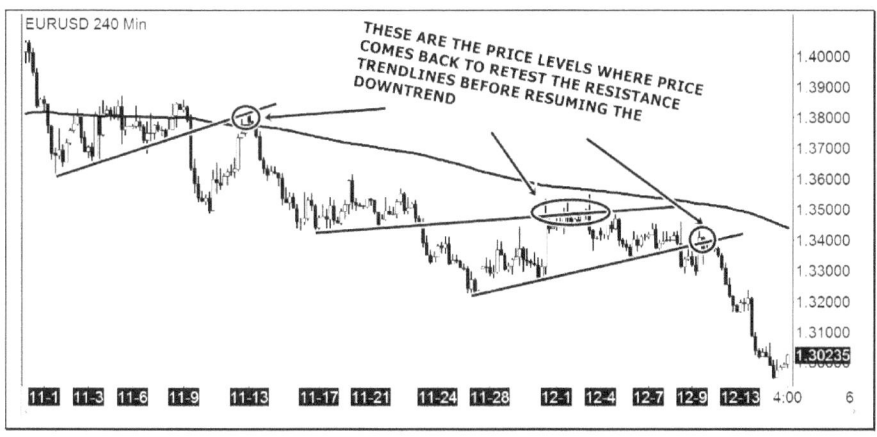

You can see that each time the support was broken to the downside, it turned into resistance as price gets back up to retest/touch the trend line previously drawn. It will not always touch the trend line like in the examples above; sometimes it will get near it and then resume the trend without a touch.

This is also a retest. In the diagram above where we have a clear downtrend and resistance levels in place, we also have now retest movements. After this point we will be looking for big bearish candlesticks with big bodies and with no/small wick at the close to signify that the sellers have entered into the market again to push the price further down and extend the trend.

Let us look at the same chart again but this time focusing

on what happens after the retest.

This is the first resistance level out of those three. There is a touch of the resistance trend line made by that big bullish hollow/white candle. After this price makes 4 very small candles that tell us this level of price is a key level where buyers have a very hard time trying to push the price further up.

This type of candles represents indecision in the market, represents equilibrium. From the beginning of the retest, buyers had no problem pushing the price up which you can clearly see by those big consecutive bullish white candles. When price got to the resistance level, the situation changed. As the main trend was down, sellers were in control of this pair and they were just waiting for a more advantageous level to sell again and resume the downtrend. These advantageous levels are always situated at a support or resistance level. It can be horizontal support/resistance, it can be diagonal like the ones we are discussing, it can be a Fibonacci retracement level, which also acts as support and resistance, it can be the 200 period moving average on the daily chart or it can be a combination of some or all of the above.

 The important thing to remember is that these are logical points in the market where buyers or sellers are most likely to step in and resume the main trend.

Okay, after those 4 small candles that tell us the buyers are losing their power, comes a big black bearish candle, much bigger than the preceding 4. This candle has a big body compared to the preceding candles and also closes near its low.

 This candle is the footprint of the sellers coming into the market to push the price back down and resume the trend. The close of this candle is the level where you would have to sell this pair. When looking after big candles to enter the market after a retest of support/resistance it is important to always compare that candle with the preceding 2-3-4 candles. The entry candle always has to be bigger than the preceding ones, has to have a big body and close at or near the low if it is bearish or at or near its high if it is a bullish big candle that signifies the uptrend will resume.

You might think that I am exaggerating the importance of this entry candle. Well, to help you realize what it really means and why I say it is the footprint of the sellers coming into the market (in this downtrend example) you must think of these 4h candles from a time perspective. Before this big black candle in the example above there were three very small 4h candles that did not push the price up or down, it just traded there in a very small range.

When the big candle emerges, we see that the price pushed down and away from that small range. This signal candle is bigger than all of the preceding three combined and it was formed in 4 hours. The last three took 12 hours to form. This is what shows us the sellers have entered the market. In only 4 hours, they managed to move the price down more than they did in the last 12 hours. Let us see the second example:

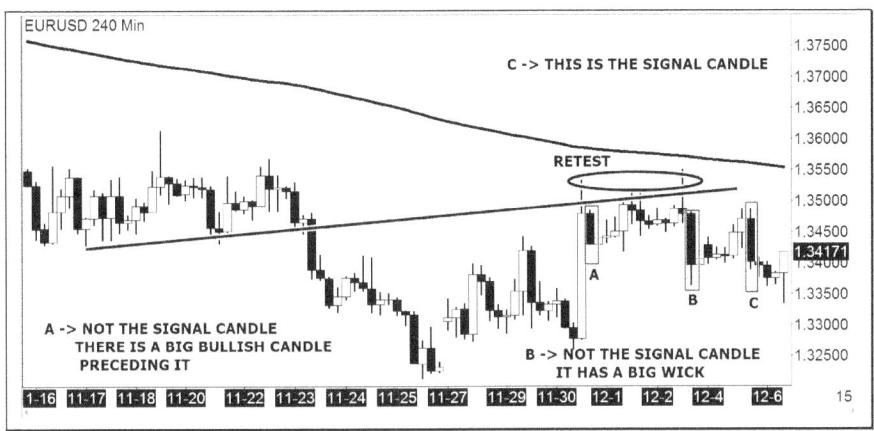

In this second example, you can see that after the retest of the resistance trend line there are three bearish candles with decent body size, which would imply that sellers have stepped into the market again.

However, the first candle (A) of these three is preceded by a huge bullish white candle. This is not our signal to sell.

The second one(B) is bigger than the first and also has no big candles preceding it. However, you can see that it does not close at or near its low, it has a big wick there, price has retraced from the low of this candle and closed almost at its middle.

This does not give us the momentum we want when entering a trade. Finally, the third candle meets our requirements; therefore, we enter the short trade at the close of this candle.

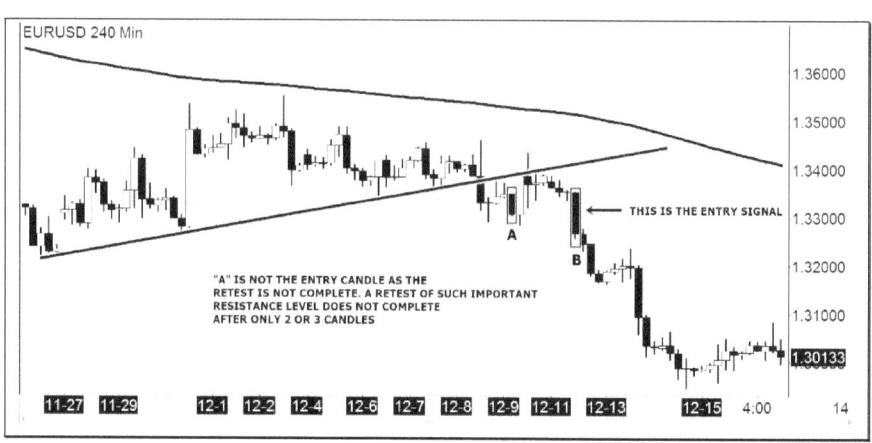

This third example is a very interesting one because it brings up an important point about retest movements of support and resistance levels.

You see here that after price breaks the trend line to the downside, it comes back up very quickly to retest it, a trend line that has now turned into resistance, and then it makes a bearish black candle that could mean sellers have entered the market.

However, this is the 4h chart, this resistance line holds great significance, it took quite some time to develop, and a lot of 4h candles, the retest absolutely has to be bigger than two 4h candles. This is why you would have to disregard that first black candle as a signal to sell. It comes way too early; the retest has to be bigger two candles. If this would have been the 5 minutes or the 15 minutes chart, and the resistance level developed in 3 hours or so then yes, the retest could have been composed of just two candles.

Still, this is a very important resistance on the 4h chart that took days to develop; the retest will more than likely be bigger than two candles.

After this black candle, we see that there are additional candles that just stagnate around that area completing the retest of the resistance level.

Finally, we have a valid signal candle that indeed pushes the price way down(B).

STOP LOSS MANAGEMENT AND TAKE PROFIT LEVELS

Now that you know how and when to enter a trade let us discuss about where to set your stop loss levels, how to trail them manually, and how to determine your ideal take profit levels. The initial stop loss level that you set when entering the trade has to always be set at above or below the level where the retest of the support/resistance ends. After this, when price goes in your favor you trail manually your stop loss above or below every swing/turning point/minor support or resistance price makes. In addition to this, you will also be determining your take profit level before you actually enter into the trade.

This is very important from the money management perspective because there will be some rare occasions when after calculating your take profit and stop loss level before entering the trade you will find that the risk you will be taking with that trade is greater than the potential reward.

Otherwise said, you would have to risk losing more pips than you could potentially win with that particular trade. The risk-reward ratio in this case is not a satisfactory one.

When you find trades like this...DO NOT TRADE. Wait for the next opportunity. Money management makes you profitable in the long run; always keep this in mind. Be very disciplined when analyzing charts and entering trades.

Always treat trading as a business and not as a game. Let us see an example of how to manage the stop loss and take profit levels.

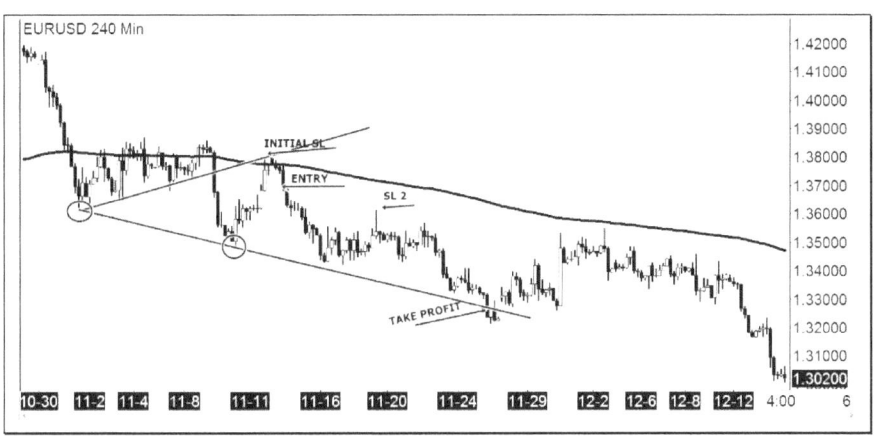

This is that first resistance level we talked about. Before entering the trade at the close of the signal black candle, you predetermine your take profit level in the following way: join with a trend line two points, the first swing of the resistance trend line and the point where the retest movement started.

The first swing of the resistance is the upper circle in this chart and the start of the retest is the second circle.

After this, extend this trend line down, and where the future price action will touch it, that is your take profit and the level where you exit the trade.

The stop loss will be set initially where the retest finished like shown in this chart and after this, as price progresses down it gives you logical turning points in the market where you can trail the stop loss (SL2).

Also in this example, you can see before entering the trade that the risk is far less than the reward. This was a 420 pips winning trade.

In this second example, the trend line for the take profit level extends far out of reach for the current price but, as long as the reward is greater than the risk(and it is), you will have no problem in entering the trade and trailing your stop loss above every turning point until it finally gets hit.

This trade actually went more in favor than this chart can illustrate and managed 550 pips of profit.

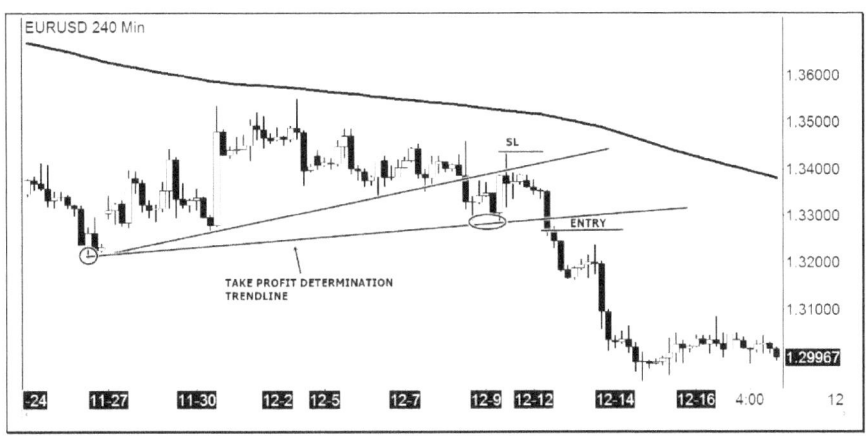

This is the example with that small retest. Before entering the trade, you draw the trend line to find out where your potential take profit will be and you see that you would have to exit the trade before you even enter it which is of course non-sense.

In addition, if that trend line would have been 10 pips lower and you would have had the chance to enter the trade, this was still not a good trade because the risk would have been greater than the 10 pips reward. Stay out of trades like this one.

There will be plenty of opportunities, this kind of trades happen frequently. An alternative way to predetermine your take profit level when the first method renders the trade unsatisfactory because of the high risk and low reward is the following:

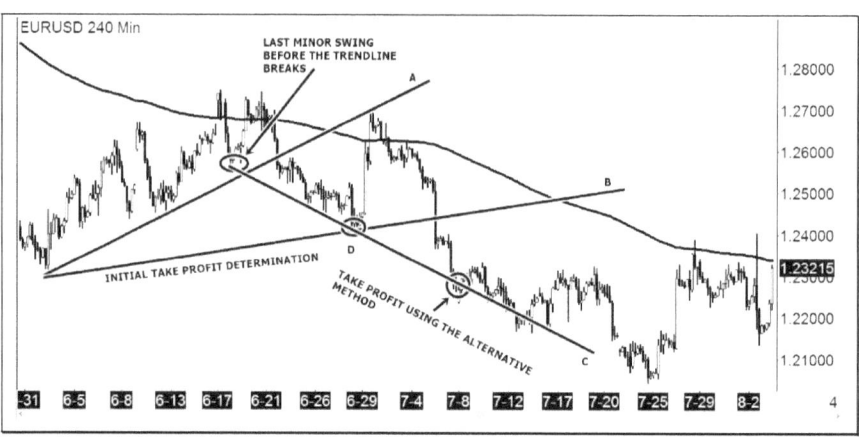

Connect with a trend line the last minor swing the pair made before the trend line(A) was broken to the downside (in the case of a downtrend) and the same start of the retest move(D circle).

Use whichever method gives you a better take profit level as long as it is not exaggerated and you think there are extremely low chances that the market will actually go to that level. If this method also does not help you achieve a good risk-reward ratio, then ignore the trade completely.

A second method that you can use to take advantage of the fact that every support becomes a resistance and every resistance becomes a support level after they have been broken it to use the same rules as with the method above, but applying them to horizontal support and resistance zones this time. However, with the diagonal support and resistance zones you have seen that they are formed by connecting two or more distinct swings in the market. With the horizontal levels, often times, you will not have a second distinct swing that you can use to draw a horizontal line. Knowing this, you must leave the candlestick chart and go to the same 4-hours chart, but a bar chart this time, and zoom it out completely.

Let me show you an example of this.

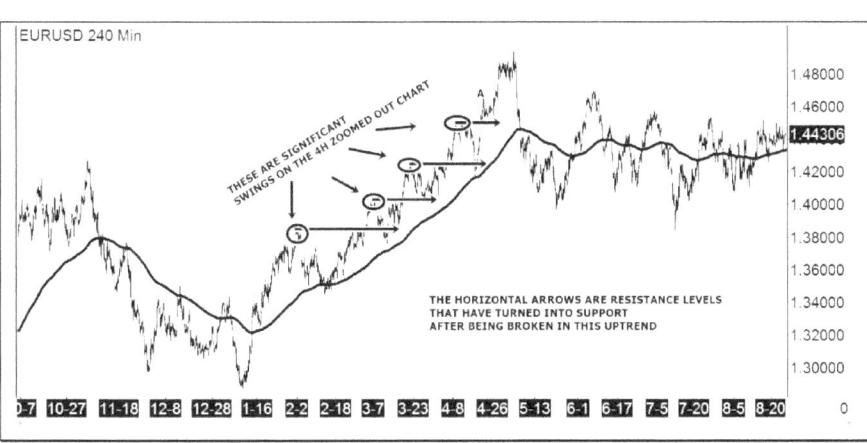

Please note that these horizontal levels come into existence just by drawing an extended horizontal line at the level where the important swings in the market are. If you want to trade the retest of these levels successfully, you have to make sure initially that they hold great importance to the overall movements of your particular forex pair. A way to make sure of this is by zooming out completely the chart like in the example above to see the big picture of the price action movements.

This way, you can put your support or resistance level into context, you can judge by looking at the surrounding price action if a swing is indeed important or not.

For example, in the chart above, after the last horizontal level, there is a minor swing that price has made there(A). You can see that I have not considered it as I think that this swing is smaller than the preceding ones on this pair and it does not hold great significance to the overall context of this pair.

Size of the swings matters. The small one is important on a lower timeframe, not on the 4 hours.

After you identify these meaningful horizontal levels, you will have no problem trading a retest of them, exactly like in the method above with the diagonal support and resistance areas. Let us see an example:

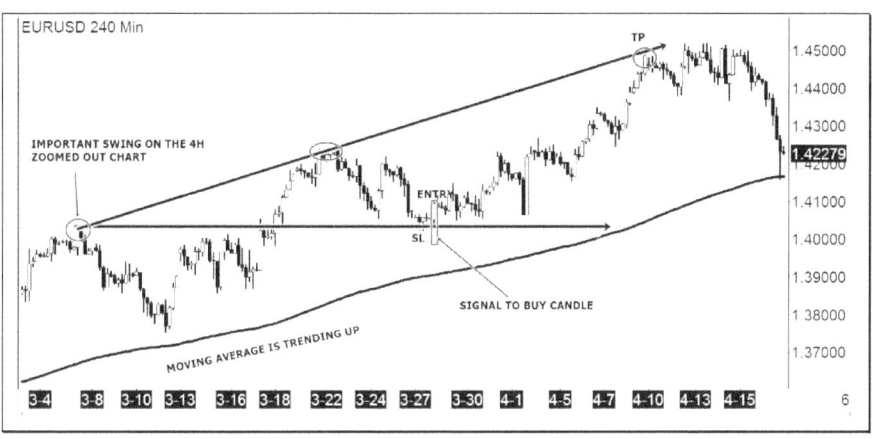

As you can see, things are clear in this trade example. The moving average is sloping up and the pair is trading above it. There is a clear uptrend.

You zoom out the chart and you find that this swing is actually quite significant by looking at the big picture.

You draw the extended horizontal line and you go back to the candlestick zoomed in chart to wait for the retest to take place(which is what this chart is showing).

The retest does indeed happen right at the horizontal support level and soon enough, you have a confirmation that the buyers have entered into the market again at this level and they are most likely to push the price upwards and extend the uptrend.

The confirmation is represented by that big, white, bullish candle that is also your signal candle to enter a buy order. The buy order is opened at the close of the signal candle of course. Trade management (stop loss and take profit) is made exactly like with the diagonal levels method.

PRICE ACTION BREAKDOWN AND IN DEPTH GUIDE TO PRICE ACTION TRADING ARE THE LATEST BOOKS THAT I HAVE WRITTEN. THEY ARE VERY POPULAR, CONSTANTLY BEING IN THE TOP 10 ON AMAZON, IN THEIR CATEGORY. PRICE ACTION BREAKDOWN WAS NUMBER ONE ON ITS CATEGORY FOR A YEAR WHEN IT WAS AVAILABLE TO READERS WHO SUBSCRIBE TO THE KINDLE UNLIMITED PROGRAM. EVEN AFTER GOING OUT OF KINDLE UNLIMITED, STILL MANAGES TO GO TO NUMBER ONE FROM TIME TO TIME.

IN AN EFFORT TO PERSUADE YOU TO EXPRESS YOUR OPINION ABOUT THE BOOK/BOOKS PUBLICLY SO THAT OTHER READERS CAN MAKE MORE INFORMED PURCHASING DECISIONS, I WOULD LIKE TO MAKE THE FOLLOWING PROPOSAL : IF YOU DO PURCHASE THE KINDLE VERSION OF ONE OR BOTH OF MY LATEST BOOKS MENTIONED ABOVE, I WOULD KINDLY ASK YOU TO REVIEW THEM ON AMAZON AFTER READING. IN EXCHANGE FOR YOU TAKING THE TIME TO WRITE A REVIEW WITH YOUR OPINION ABOUT THE BOOK/BOOKS, I WOULD LIKE TO MAKE AN OFFER.

FOR ONE VERIFIED PURCHASE REVIEW YOU WRITE ON ANY OF THE 2 BOOKS ABOVE, I CAN OFFER THE PDF VERSION OF THE REVIEWED BOOK, THE PDF VERSION OF THIS BOOK YOU ARE CURRENTLY READING, PLUS ONE OTHER BOOK OF MINE (ALSO IN PDF VERSION), AT YOUR CHOOSING, FROM THE ONES I WROTE IN 2012 (THIS INCLUDES ALL BUT THE TWO IN QUESTION).

IF YOU DECIDE TO FOLLOW THROUGH ON THIS OFFER, AFTER THE REVIEW HAS BEEN COMPLETED, PLEASE EMAIL ME AT LAURENTIUDAMIR@GMAIL.COM, SPECIFY ON WHAT AMAZON WEBSITE HAS THE REVIEW BEEN POSTED, UNDER WHAT USER NAME AND WHAT OTHER BOOK OF MINE WOULD YOU LIKE TO RECEIVE IN PDF FORMAT, BESIDES THE REVIEWED ONE AND THE ONE YOU ARE CURRENTLY READING

In the end I would like to apologize if I sound a little rigid in my explanations and if there are any misspellings. English is not my first language. I am doing the best I can.

If you find that this adds value to your trading please consider writing a review of the book on Amazon. It does not have to be long, just a few words to state your opinion about the trading system presented in order to help other people make more informed decisions.

Thank you for reading this book and happy forex trading. Hope you found it valuable.

FOLLOW PRICE ACTION TRENDS STRATEGY

TABLE OF CONTENTS

INTRODUCTION

This is a forex system based solely on reading the price action. It is a trend following system that focuses on points in the market where the trend is about to change its direction, enters the market trying to ride the newly formed trend all the way to its finish line.

By doing this in the correct way, this system has the potential to deliver thousands of pips in the long run because shortly after a trend ends, usually another one emerges preceded by a small period of consolidation.

It sounds simple, but the key component of this price action system is to correctly identify the current trend, know when a change in direction of the trend is about to take place and then manage the new developing trend in a way that allows you to ride it until it ends.

All of this is done by carefully reading the price action without the use of any technical indicators, magical formulas and other nonsense like that.

This is not a very easy thing to do as you must pay great

attention to every single detail of the price action, but once you get the hang of it trading this way will make you very profitable in the long run.

This book explains with very great detail all of the above and gives you the complete trading system with clear entry, stop loss and exit rules, rules that if respected to the letter, can bring you hundreds of pips for every trade you make.

Let us move on now to the core part of this forex system which is the trend.

TREND

You've probably heard a million times by now the saying "the trend is your friend".

Well, you've heard it because it is true, if you want to be profitable in trading you must always know what the trend is because the trend signifies strong conviction from the vast majority of market participants that the fair price, fair value of a specific currency pair should be above or below the current level at that time so they all join forces and push the price up or down creating a trend this way.

But let us see what a trend actually is from a technical point of view.

A trend is a series of impulsive strong moves in one direction, each of them followed by small corrections or retracements. Let's visualize a textbook trend:

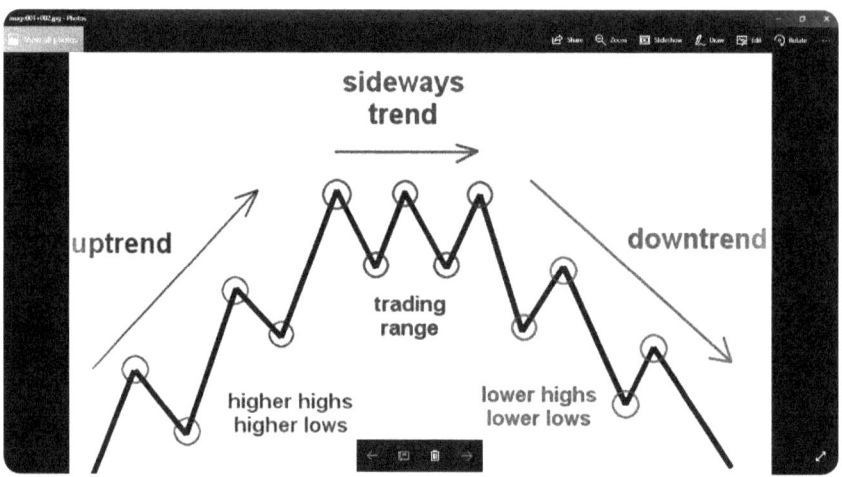

We have in the above picture an ideal uptrend and a downtrend. As you can see they consist of strong directional moves followed by smaller moves in the opposite direction which are in fact formed by traders taking some profit from their positions.

This alternation of impulsive moves with correctional ones gives birth to what are known as the highs and lows of a trend.

For an uptrend the high is formed when the correctional move starts and the low is where the same move ends and price resumes the trend.

For a downtrend things work the other way around meaning that a low is formed at the beginning of a correction and a high takes form at the end of the same correction and price resumes the downtrend.

In the example above you can see that these highs and lows can easily be connected with a trend line.

So, to conclude this, we have an uptrend when the price starts to make higher highs (HH) and higher lows (HL) and we have a downtrend when price is making lower highs (LH) and lower lows (LL) just like in the pictures above.

Unfortunately, trends so simple and clear like those above are very rare in real market conditions.

Let's see some real trends:

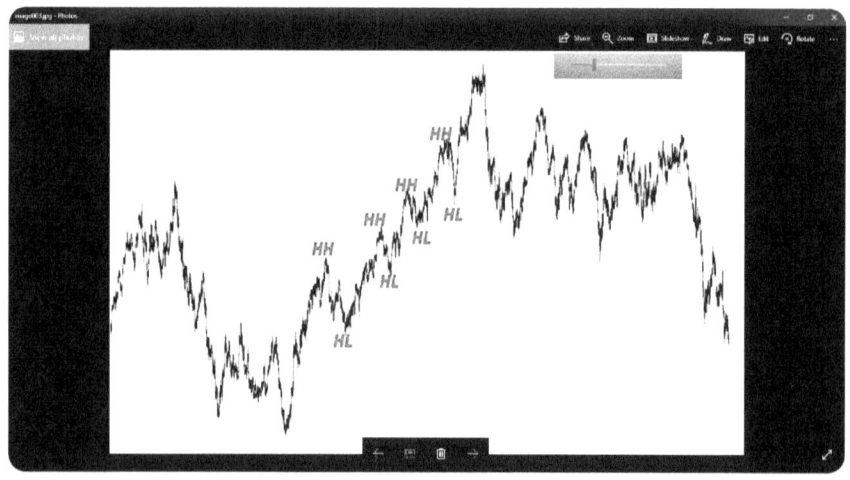

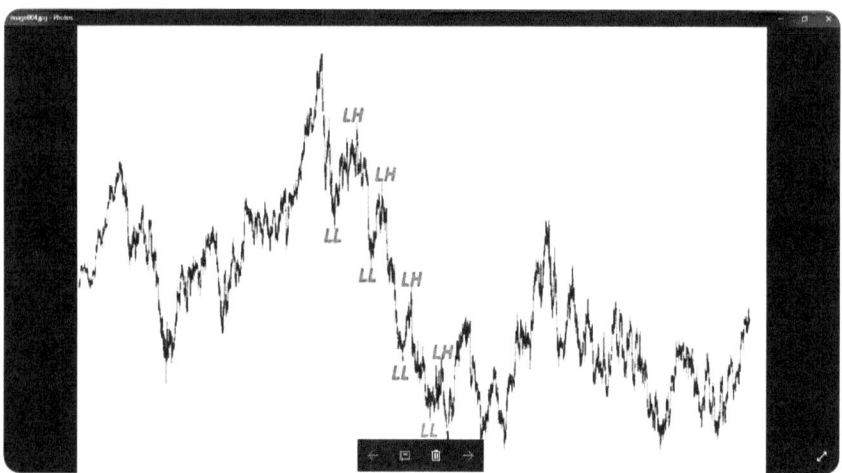

We have above one uptrend and one downtrend. This is just about the closest that real market trends can get to resemble those ideal textbook trends.

It doesn't get any easier than this in real market conditions. However, trends like these two above are rare especially in the forex market which is known to be a very volatile market. Even in these clear trends you can see that there are some variations, there are some smaller trends contained in the bigger trend.

Let's see now how a more common trend for the forex market can look like:

This is a downtrend but you can tell it is more complicated than the previous ones just by looking at it.

There are some important rules I designed to help you correctly identify and mark the components of a trend. Here is the first one.

CORRECTIONS

Corrections or retracements can also exist in the form of a trading range that has an upper and a lower boundary where price stalls for a period of time and takes a breath before resuming the trend.

As you learned before, a correction move happens when traders start to take some profit out from the market and, as a consequence of that, price goes for a short period of time in the opposite direction only to resume the trend later on.

In this particular example we have a downtrend and the

people that are short are starting to take profits.

When these sellers start to do this, the people that are convinced that this pair will go upwards from here decide that this is a good level for them to buy this pair.

So, in general, a correction move begins because some traders decide to mark some profits and at the same time other traders enter the market in the opposite direction. In the case above, there weren't many people buying this pair at the level where the correction started to unfold and so price did not make a classic correction.

When a correction looks like a consolidation range it means that the current trend in very strong and it is very likely that it will continue further.

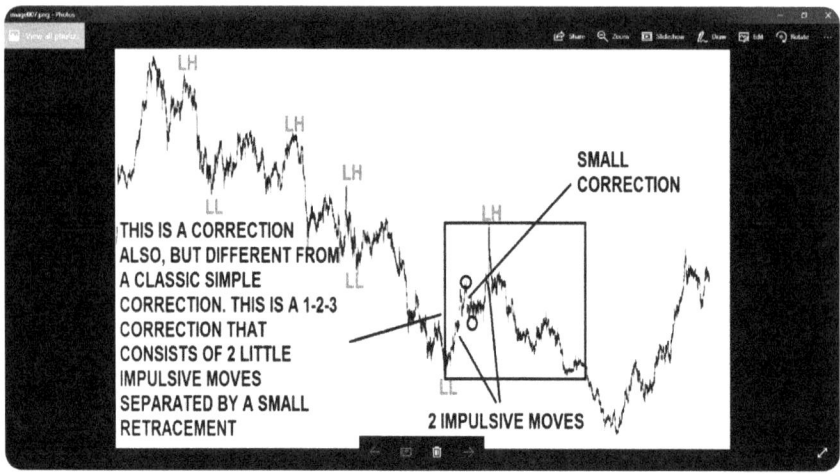

In the above example you can see that in the same trend further down we have a different form of correction that basically has its own highs and lows.

It has a first impulsive move opposite to the trend direction and at that point you could very well say that this is a classic correction but, as you can see it makes a small correction and then another impulsive move upwards.

Because this correction has its own highs and lows you could make the mistake to consider it as a trend change. However, it stays very well confined into the territory of the last impulsive move down of our trend. It stays well below the last lower high of our trend so it is still a correction even if it develops a higher high.

But you will learn more about this we get to the change of

trend section.

Corrections can take a lot of forms, these are just the most common ones, the important thing to remember is that for a correction move to be valid it must not be bigger than its impulsive move, it must not surpass the beginning of the impulsive move.

Let's see some examples:

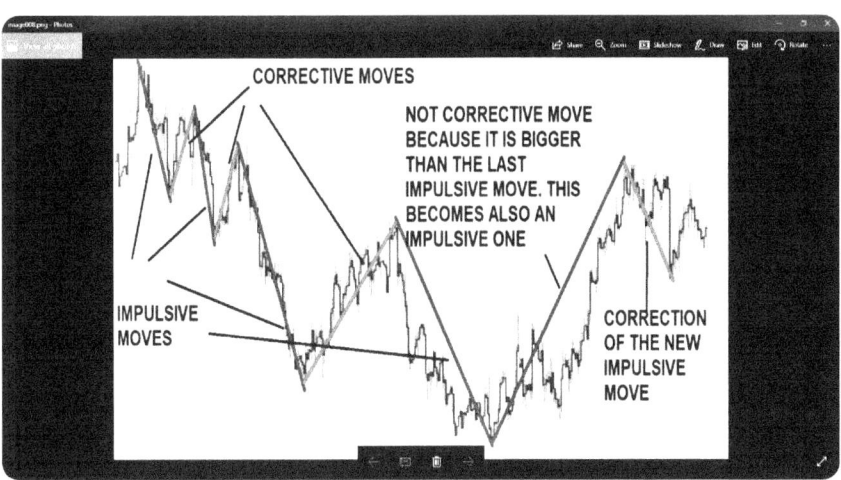

You can see on this chart that the correction move has to always be smaller than the last impulsive move. At the bottom of the chart you see an impulsive move but it is followed by a larger move in the opposite direction so that cannot be considered a correction.

This is how a trend usually changes direction but we will learn more about this later on.

Okay, I think it is pretty clear what a correction is by now it is not hard at all to see it. Now let us go to the second important rule of a trend and that has to do with correctly identifying highs and lows.

CONFIRMATION

The rule is that any high or low must be confirmed by the subsequent price action.

We know from the above pages that highs and lows are formed at the beginning and finish of a correction move but, for those highs and lows to be valid price has to make another strong impulsive move in the direction of the trend.

By strong impulsive move I mean price has to go well beyond the beginning of the correctional move that made these potential highs and lows.

Only after this strong impulsive move happens we can label those potential highs and lows as new valid, confirmed highs and lows in our trend.

If this impulsive move does not happen or it is not strong then our potential highs and lows are not confirmed, they are not valid.

Valid highs and lows remain the previous ones that have been confirmed by subsequent price action. Let's see a chart so you can better understand this:

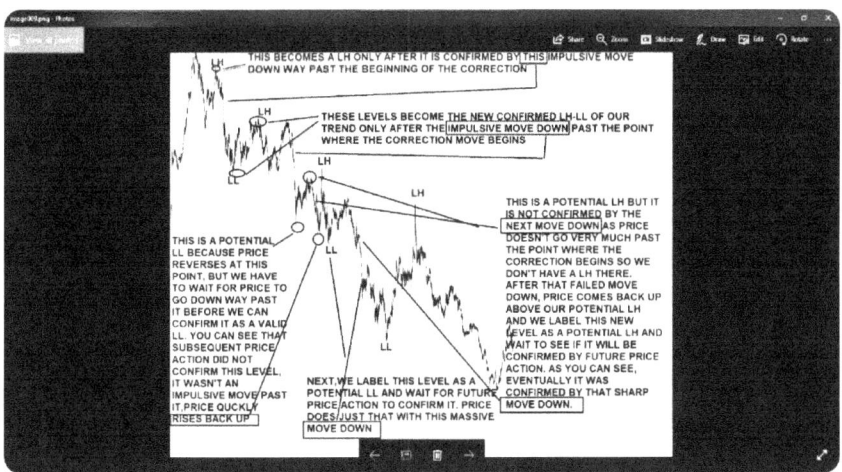

You can see in this chart above that what we have to do to correctly identify the highs and lows of our trend.

As the trend unfolds in real time we mark every level where there has been a change in direction as a potential highs or low and then we wait for the next impulsive move down, in this case, to tell us if our potential high/low has been confirmed and it is valid. If the next move down doesn't go well past the start of the correction then we disregard these levels that we marked as potential high/low and we wait for price action to make its next move and show us where the new and confirmed high and low will be.

Let us see another example:

Here we have an uptrend , price makes two HH and two HL and then when it looks like it is preparing to make the third pair of HH-HL the pair starts a series of quick up and down moves almost equal in length.

None of these can be considered as a new HH-HL because price doesn't go up at all, it just stays there and consolidates and so we do not have a new pair of HH-HL here. After this you can see that price does go up with a pretty strong move past the point where correction began but doesn't go far and retraces back down. We still don't have a confirmed pair of new HH-HL.

In the end, finally price goes very strongly upwards with a massive impulsive move, thus confirming our trend's new HL and HH.

Things like this are pretty tricky to manage in real time but with the help of this book and with practice it will become easy in time. Let's see some other examples:

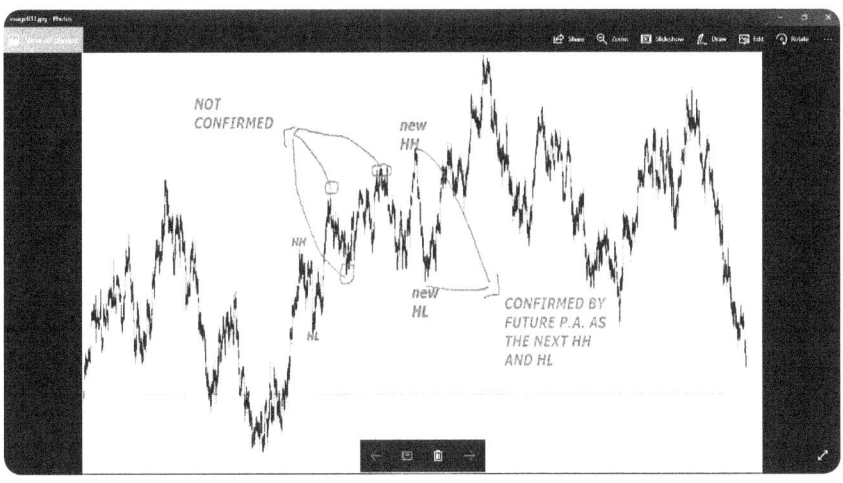

In the chart above we have the same situation as in the previous chart.

Okay, now let's see a more complicated one:

In the downtrend above you can see that we have a strange trend that has the first and the last two pairs of LH-LL very close to each other.

You saw in the earlier examples that we disregard our potential highs and lows if the next impulsive move does not go past the starting point of the correction move or it goes past just slightly.

In situations like in the chart above where things are somewhere in a gray area, meaning that the impulsive move goes past a little bit more than slightly but still not enough to confirm the pair of LH-LL, we do not disregard this pair of LH-LL, we take note of it and after the price makes another pair of potential LH-LL and it is finally confirmed by a strong impulsive move, we label the first pair as well as LH-LL.

So we have two pairs of LH-LL close to each other in situations like these two in the chart above. Let me explain better so you can understand when to disregard a pair and when not to.

From my experience I have come to the conclusion that the impulsive move that comes after a correction to continue the trend has to have the length, size of approximately two times that of the correction move for me to consider it as a strong impulsive move that confirms and validates any potential high or low.

Remember: strong impulsive move is a move with the length of approximately 2 times that of the correction or more. Moderate impulsive moves are those two in the last example where we had to lable 2 pairs of LH-LL close to each other.

Let's go to that chart again and see what was the size of these moves with respect to their preceding corrections:

This is the the same chart with the same trend but it is zoomed in so you can better see what is going on with those first 2 pairs of LH-LL we talked about.

You can see the correction move has a span of approximately 260 pips and moderate move down as I call it is 380 pips in length. This means it surpasses the start of the correction by almost have of the correction move length.

If the amplitude of the move down would have been 500 pips or so then this would've been a strong correction move and we would have labeled the first pair of LH-LL right after the move, we wouldn't have to wait for that huge move down after the second pair.

Let's see on the same trend the last two pairs of LH-LL

which have identical dynamics as these first two:

Here the impulsive move is not that big compared to the correction move like in the previous example but it is still 30% bigger in length so this is also a moderate impulsive move.

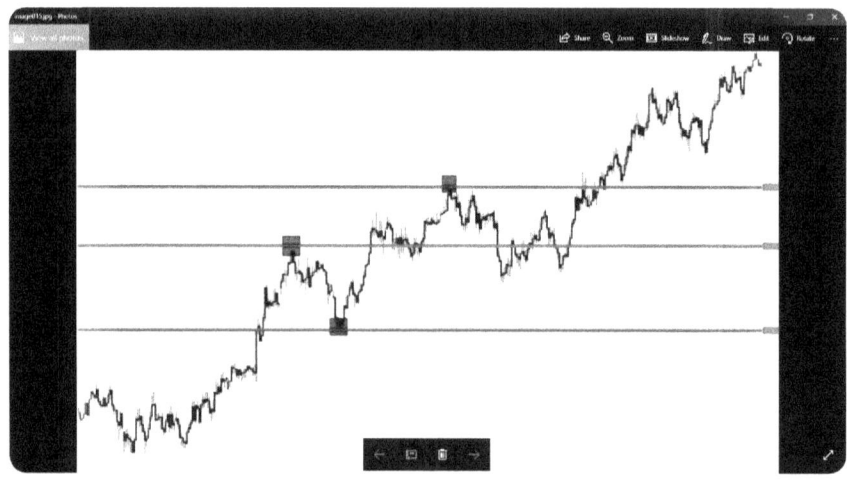

Here is another moderate impulsive move.

And another one:

And yet another. You can see here that the sebsequent strong move down never came so our potential pair of LL-LH was never confirmed.

This is a strong impulsive move down, it is almost two times bigger than the correction in length.

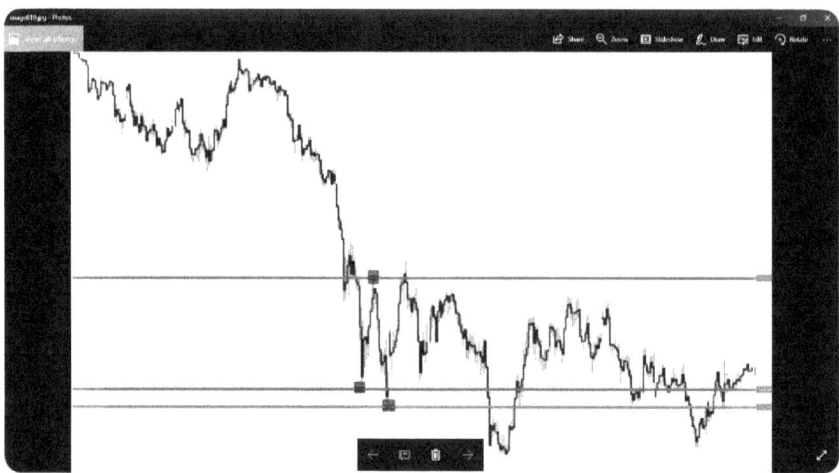

This is a very small impulsive move that passes the start of the correction by only a few pips. We definitely do not have a pair of LH-LL here.

We don't have a pair here either. We disconsider those potential LH and LL.

You can see this was a very goog thing to do as price later rose back up and passed our potential LH by a few pips.

We will see later when we get to the stop loss placement why this is important.

The exact same thing happened in the previous example.

This example is one of the best as you can see a series of potential pairs of HL-HH that were never confirmed and had to be disregarded as the move upwards right after each one of them was not strong at all and not even moderate.

Okay, I think you have a clear idea now on how to correctly label the highs and lows of a trend. After reading all this, you should pull up a chart and start to practice on past price action.

Let us go now to the third important rule of a trend which is the degree. This is perhaps the most important part when trying to correctly identify the highs and lows of a trend.

THE DEGREE

You've learned by now that a trend is composed of impulsive moves and their corresponding corrective moves.

Let's put together the impulsive move with its corresponding correction move and call it a wave, like in the charts below:

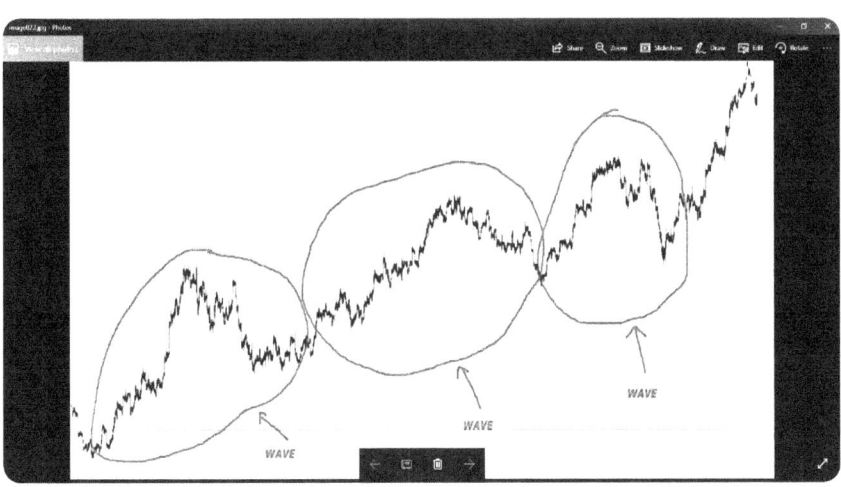

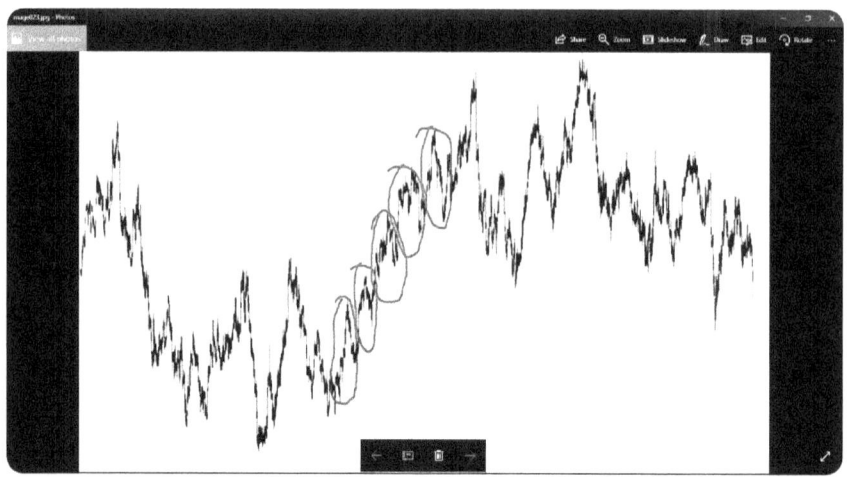

When trying to identify the correct highs and lows of the trend that are basically formed by these waves you have to make sure first that the waves you want to mark as a pair of high-low are of approximately the same degree, measure, extent, amplitude, size like these in the above charts.

Look at the following chart:

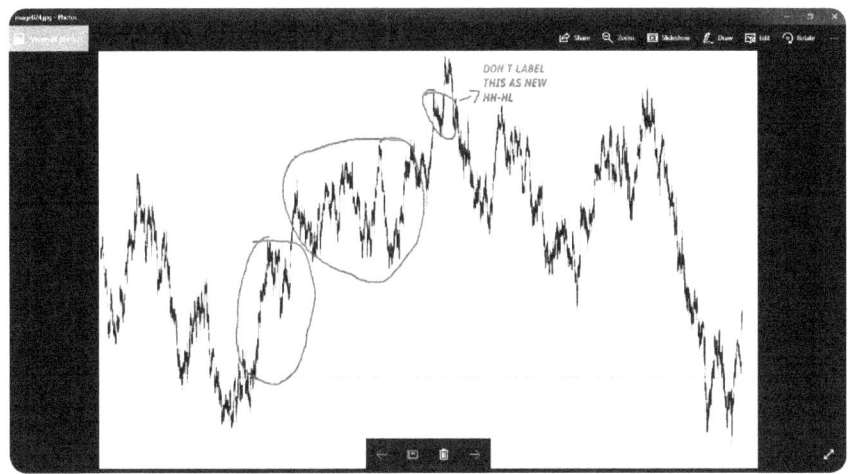

We have two big waves followed by a very small wave compared to the first two. This is not of the same degree or size as the first two.

Do not consider this pair the new HH and HL. You wait for a wave of about the same amplitude to label as new HH and HL.

If it does not come like it happened with the trend in this chart, the last pair of HH-HL remains that of the last big wave.

Another example like the one above:

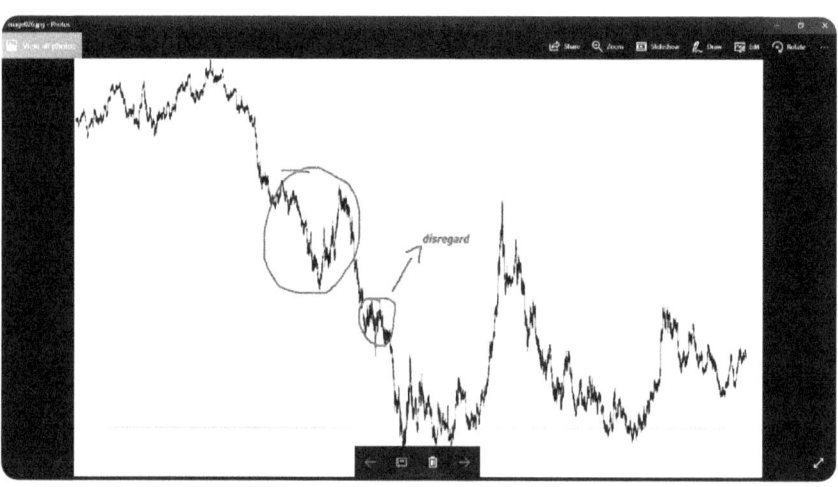

And another one:

Yet another one.

As you can see in these examples this is not exact science, but with practice you will easily know what to label and what not.

Okay know you have a very good idea of how to identify the trend, how to identify its corrections and impulsive moves, how to correctly label the highs and lows taking into account the subsequent price action movement and the degree of the waves that form the trend.

TREND CHANGE

In short, a trend changes direction when price action makes a wave in the opposite direction of the trend near the zone of the last lower high of a downtrend or the last higher low of an uptrend.

The trend is considered to have reversed its direction when, after the wave in opposite direction, price action penetrates that last lower high in a downtrend or the last higher low in an uptrend. Let us see an example:

We have a downtrend here.

The horizontal line is where the last lower high of the downtrend is placed. Price makes an impulsive move upwards that penetrates the last LH and then a small correction.

The impulsive and corrective move put together are the wave near the last lower high I talked about just earlier. When this small correction finishes and price comes back up passing the start of the correction is when the trend changes from downtrend to uptrend. This is the exact place where we will enter our trades. Let's see more examples of trend changes:

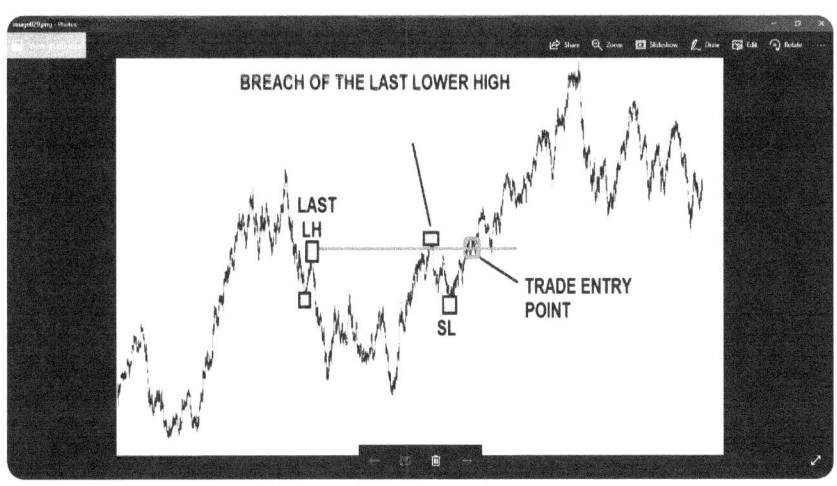

The same thing happens here.

Last LH gets penetrated and price continues upwards after a small correction. You can see from this chart where we will enter our trade and also where do we set our initial stop loss.

As a rule, the initial stop loss will always be placed like in the chart above, at the level where correction ends, preceding the price move past the breach of last LH/HL level.

The entry level has variations but in this example we enter a buy stop order at the level shown in the chart, after we see that price starts to make a correction at that level.

In this example we have a different situation.

The wave in the opposite direction does not breach the last lower high but it is in the zone of it. In this case we enter the buy stop order right after price comes up after the correction and passes the level of the last lower high.

Remember, in this situation we don't enter the trade at the start of the correction because that level is still below the last LH, it did not breach the LH like in the examples above.

These are the only two situations where we have to manage our entry point.

If the wave breaches the last LH/HL we enter at the start of the correction because that level already penetrated the LH/HL. If the wave does not breach the last LH/HL like in the example above, we enter the trade as explained above and shown in the chart.

Another example:

Uptrend changes into a downtrend.

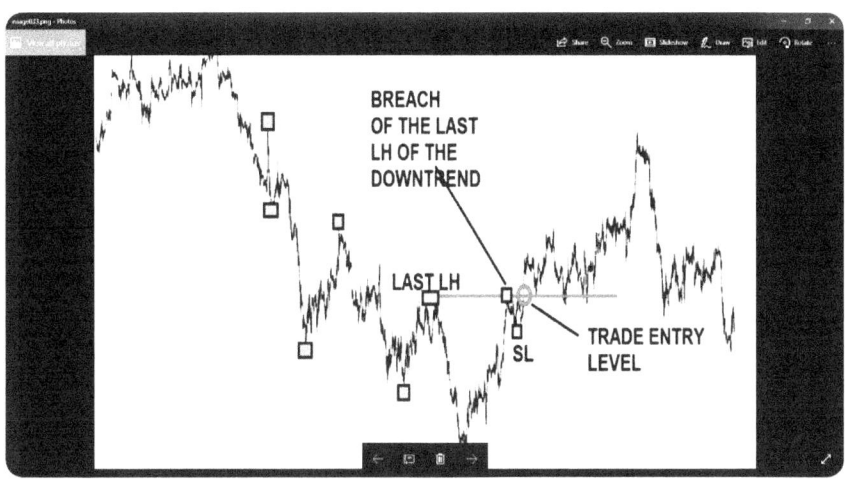

You have here another example of a trend change.

Now let's see how we manage our stop loss level so we can get as many pips as we can out of every trade we make.

The stop loss will be trailed manually under every valid HL if we are buying and above every valid LH if we are selling.

TRADE SETUP

We will enter trades based on the trend of the 1 hour chart zoomed out to the maximum.

This is the most suitable time frame for this strategy because the trend here changes direction frequently, therefore you will be in the market 80-90% of the time using this timeframe and you will not have to hold a trade open for weeks as you would do if you traded with this method on the 4h chart or the daily one.

I am not saying not to trade on a higher time frame with this system, in fact that will be more productive in the long term, I am saying stick with the 1h chart if you do not have it in you to hold a trade open for weeks at a time.

Now, there is a very important rule here: when the trend changes like in the examples above, before we enter a trade in any direction, we always make sure that the trend on the 4 hours timeframe is in the same direction that we will enter our trade in on the   hour chart.

Always remember this rule. Let me show you what happens if you do not respect this rule:

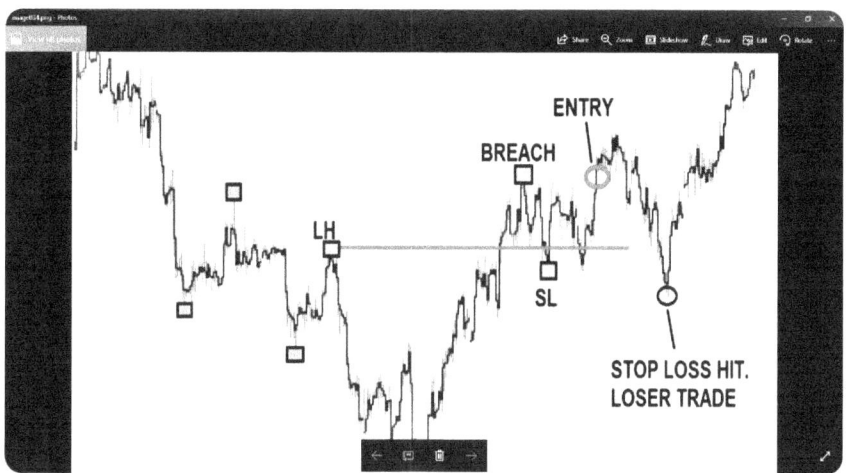

Trend changes from down to up, we enter, set the stop loss, price goes just slightly in our favor and then retraces quickly and hits our stop loss.

Why? Look as this:

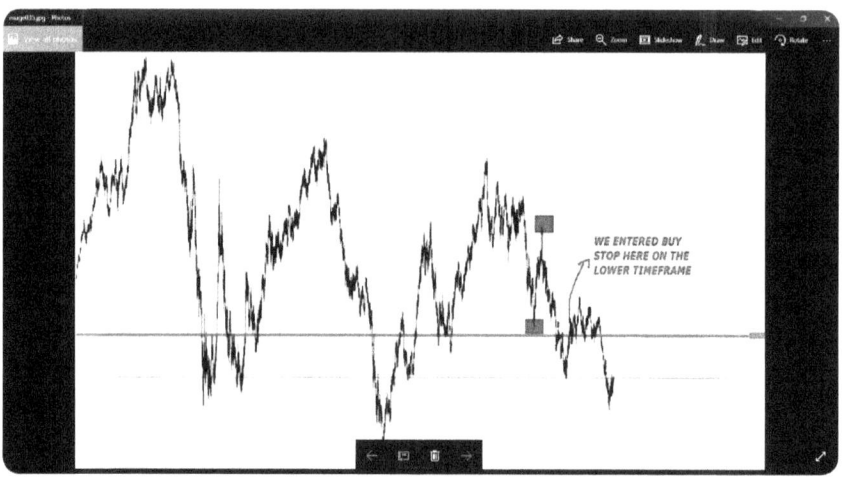

This is the bigger timeframe chart. You can see that here the trend is clearly down.

Always look at the 4h chart to confirm that the trend there is in the direction of the trade you are about to enter on the 1h chart.

TRADING SYSTEM STEP BY STEP

Go to the 1h completely zoomed out chart and find the trend using what you learned here. Don't be shallow with this part of chart analysis. Be very meticulous, this step is the most important.

Wait for this trend to change like discussed in the trend change section.

When the trade setup happens go to the 4h chart and make sure that the trend on that timeframe has the same direction as the trade you are about to enter on the 1h chart. If this is not the case, do not enter the trade.

If the 4h timeframe trend confirms your trade direction enter the trade on the 1h chart and set your initial stop loss level like discussed above.

Trail your stop loss manually below every valid HL that the new uptrend makes or above every LH that the new downtrend makes.

You can also use this system to trade the changes in trend on the 4h chart with confirmation of trend direction from the daily chart and you can use it on the daily chart with confirmation of trend direction from the weekly chart.

The higher the timeframe, the bigger the profits will be.

TRADE EXAMPLES

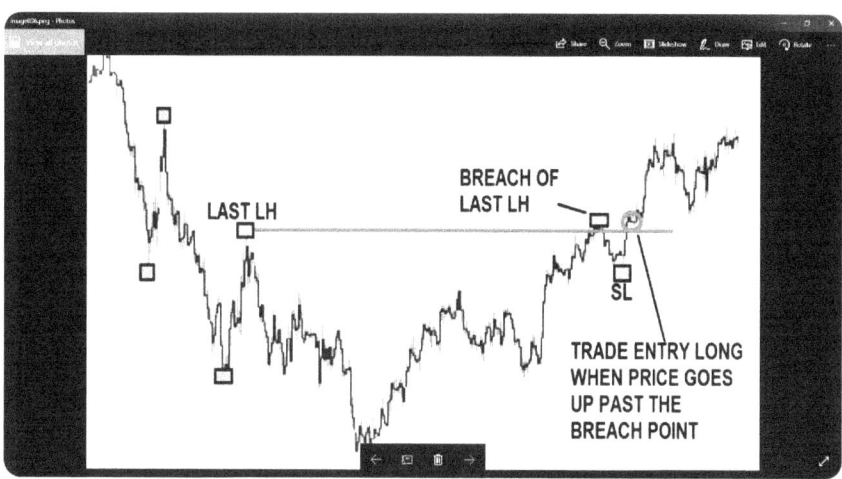

We enter the trade here on the change of the trend. Let's see what happens next:

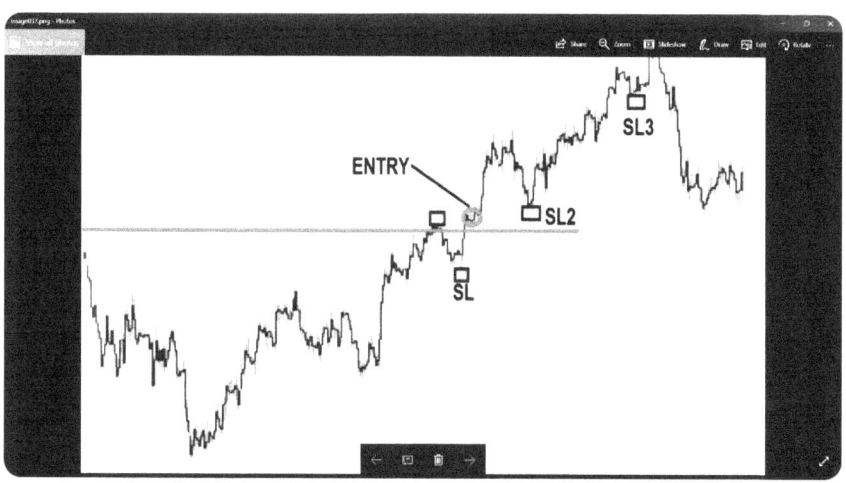

You trail the stop loss only at valid HL's. The trade ends at the SL 3 level.

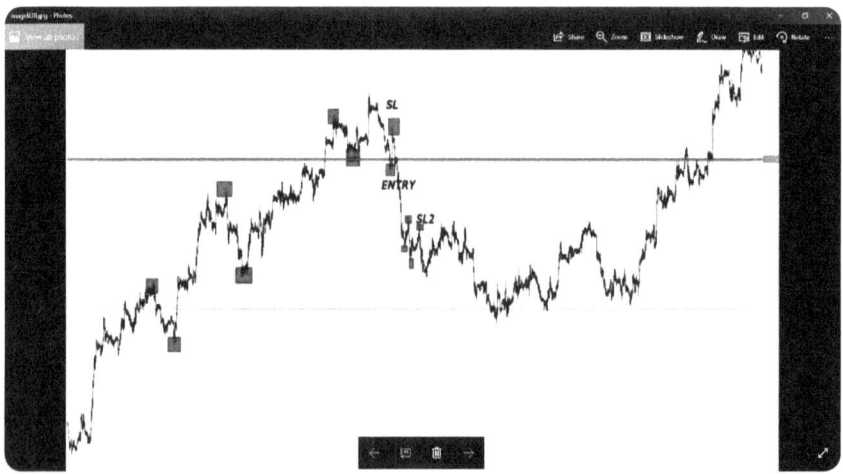

Another trade just a few hours after we exited the first, SL2 is the level we exit this one.

We exited on SL2 but the trend did not change there, it goes down a little bit more.

There is nothing we can do but wait for the trend to change. With the help of that square you can see how long we have to wait before the next change of trend occurs.

Of course, keep in mind that you always have to check the 4h trend before you enter any trade.

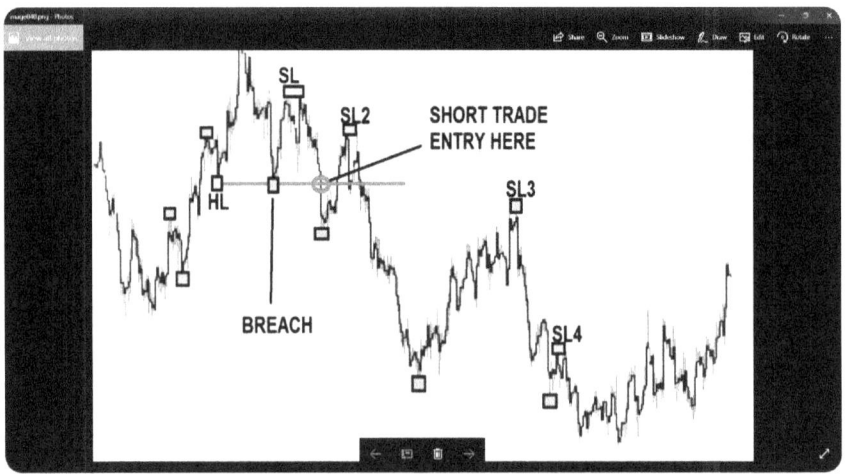

You exit at SL4 level.

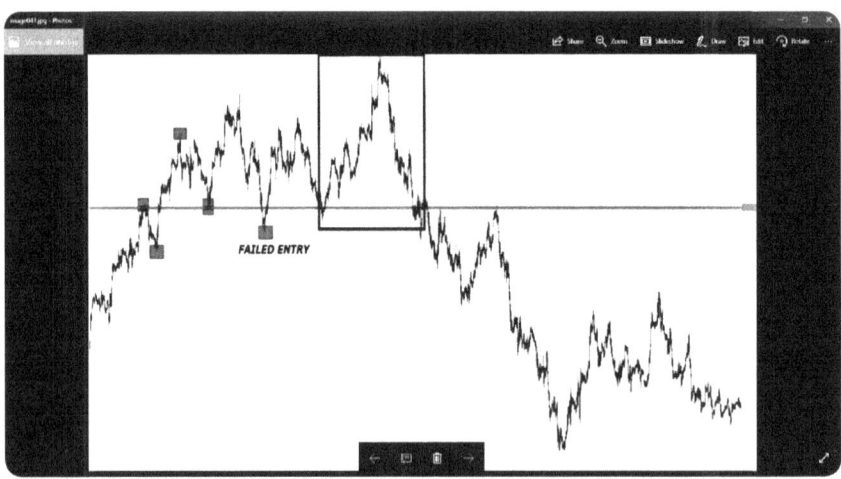

In this example you set your sell stop order at the entry level but the price fails to confirm the trend change and continues the uptrend for a while.

There is nothing you can do here.

In the end I would like to apologize if I sound a little to rigid in my explanations and if there are any misspellings. English is not my first language. I am doing the best I can.

Thank you and happy trading.

If you find that this adds value to your trading please consider writing a review of the book on Amazon. It does not have to be long, just a few words to state your opinion about the trading system presented in order to help other people make more informed decisions.